Revival Living

insights from 1 Timothy for the 3rd millennium church

Stephen Gaukroger

THE WORD MADE FRESH!

discussion starters for small groups

Revival Living: *insights from 1 Timothy for the 3rd millennium church*

A **scriptureunion@goldhill** product published by Scripture Union, 207–209 Queensway, Bletchley, MK2 2EB, UK. This imprint is especially created to bring the ministry of Gold Hill Baptist Church to a wider audience.

Scripture Union is an international Christian charity working with churches in more than 130 countries providing resources to bring the good news about Jesus Christ to children, young people and families – and to encourage them to develop spiritually through the Bible and prayer. As well as a network of volunteers, staff and associates who run holidays, church-based events and school Christian groups, SU produces a wide range of publications and supports those who use their resources through training programmes.

Email: info@scriptureunion.org.uk Internet: www.scriptureunion.org.uk

Scripture Union Australia
Locked Bag 2, Central Coast Business Centre, NSW 2252 222 Internet: www.su.org.au

Gold Hill: Gold Hill is a Baptist Church and member of the Evangelical Alliance. Their mission statement is: Equipping God's people, Serving God's Son, Reaching God's World. The church meets at Gold Hill Common East, Chalfont St Peter, SL9 9DG. Stephen Gaukroger is the senior pastor.

Email: office@goldhill.org.uk Internet: www.goldhill.org.uk

© Stephen Gaukroger 2004
First published 2004

ISBN 1 84427 042 4

All rights reserved. No part of this publication may be reproduced, stored in a retrieval system, or transmitted, in any form or by any means, electronic, mechanical, photocopying, recording or otherwise, without the prior permission of Scripture Union.

The right of Stephen Gaukroger to be identified as author of this work has been asserted by him in accordance with the Copyright, Designs and Patents Act 1988.

Quotations from the New International Version of the Holy Bible, © 1973, 1978, 1984 by International Bible Society, used by permission of Hodder and Stoughton Limited.

British Library Cataloguing-in-Publication Data: a catalogue record for this book is available from the British Library.

Cover design by aricot vert of Fleet.

Internal design by David Lund Design.

Printed and bound by Ebenezer Baylis, The Trinity Press, Worcester.

Scripture Union: Using the Bible to inspire children, young people and adults to know God

REVIVAL LIVING

Revival Living
Insights from 1 Timothy for the 3rd Millennium Church
Intro

When you get older, you are faced with some choices about how you behave. Some people in mature years become increasingly sinister and bitter, and dismissive of younger people. Here the elderly Paul, an experienced church planter, is writing to the young Timothy, just starting out in service in the church in Ephesus. It would have been so easy for him to adopt a cynical or patronising tone: 'Well, Tim, God bless you in your ministry. I suppose you know things are going to be pretty difficult?'

Remember that Paul himself might be far from comfortable as he writes. He might be in prison or he might be between prison appearances. We are not entirely sure; the book of Acts leaves us with a very incomplete story, ending a little enigmatically, just like the soap episode ending at a crucial point in the plot. The credits always start rolling just as you're about to discover whether she really is pregnant, or he really is about to confess to murder or whatever! Acts concludes by saying that the apostle Paul continued to do his stuff for two years and then … well, we're not sure.

But this letter is not a predictable literary pat on the head from someone feeling a bit sidelined or sorry for himself. Here you have an older man with the fire burning in his belly just as passionately as it did when he was younger! This is a letter about living in revival and how to do it – and it's from a man who really knows. Timothy is church planting in Ephesus and it's a struggle. Paul has seen it all before. Jesus burst into his life with a shining light on the Damascus Road and turned him around 180 degrees and sent him in another direction. He's planted churches in key towns in the ancient world – Lustra, Derbe, Antioch. He's planted congregations of living, vibrant believers. He's seen miracles and disappointments. He's preached successfully;

and seen his preaching fall on deaf ears. He's been there, done that and got the t-shirt! Yet, far from being a spent force, he is still full of joy and faith. He is still looking for revival, for God to breathe on people.

Is that our longing? Do we want the cobwebs of our spirituality and our mediocrity and our plain ordinariness to be blown away by the breath of God?

So, our scene is set. Let's learn from an old apostle and a young pastor wanting – like us – to be the best they can be for God.

Stephen Gaukroger

REVIVAL LIVING

How to get the best out of **the Word made fresh!**

This series of **the Word made fresh!** discussion starters for small groups provides thought-provoking teaching from Stephen Gaukroger with questions to stimulate discussion and prayer.

The material will suit groups wanting to think about biblical principles as they affect and challenge contemporary life – particularly groups wanting to explore all this within a fairly unstructured programme. It is suitable for newly-formed or established or mixed groups, of about six to 14 members, with limited or extensive Bible knowledge.

It will be helpful if the group leader has had some experience of leading and some understanding of group dynamics, as working with the free format of **the Word made fresh!** will be stretching. Particular attention will need to be paid to involving everyone in the discussion, and avoiding the domination of the conversation by one or two people. It will be a real asset if the group leader has spent time getting to know the members as individuals so that he or she can more readily identify topics which need particularly sensitive handling. That said, the format requires little preparation for the leader apart from a thorough reading of the teaching section and some advance thinking about the questions and Bible verses.

All group members need their own copy of this workbook. Where group members can commit to reading both the Bible passages and the study material in advance of meeting together this can be a real advantage – the group leader need only recall the main points. But if this is not practical, another approach to getting the best out of the material would be to spend 10 to 15 minutes having the study material read aloud by one or more people at the beginning of the session, perhaps in the relaxed setting of coffee and doughnuts.

The worksheet will guide discussion and is intended to be completed during the session. However, the purpose of the time together will be largely fulfilled if the group members have interacted

- with the teaching;
- with the Bible verses;
- with each other in expressing their thoughts and
- with God in prayer.

So completing the worksheet fully or neatly with the 'right' answers is not a criterion for judging the group time! Some people will find it helpful as a record of their thoughts and the discussion, while others will find it a hindrance. Feel free!

REVIVAL LIVING

Revival Living
1: Passing the torch
1 Timothy 1:1–11

It's a thrilling moment when the torch arrives in the packed stadium as the signal for the Olympic Games to begin. The torch is passed to a new generation of athletes seeking new record-breaking performances, to achieve even greater things than have been done in the past.

So with Paul and Timothy. And so with us. With God, the best is always yet to be. We thank God for the past, but honour it not by living in it but by learning from it and facing the future. We live in the expectation that the revival and blessing we may have seen historically is a pale imitation of what God will do.

From these early verses the passion in Paul's voice is evident. He is not some old codger put out to grass. From a warm personal greeting, he moves straight into some serious teaching about the issues affecting Timothy's ministry.

What does it take in a leader to make a great church? Two vital things are illustrated in combination here. It takes **personal warmth** and it takes **commitment to the truth**. Timothy is Paul's adopted son, a spiritual son, and Paul loves him. He doesn't just race into the advice for sorting out Timothy's church. No, he takes time to affirm Timothy (1:2).

A leader should make sure that within our churches there's time for the personal touch, for reminiscing, for confirming relationship. It matters that preaching the gospel is done in the context of relationship. A church should be a place where someone knows your name. It's impossible for a pastor of a large church to know everyone's name – but hopefully someone makes it their business to know your name. The church is about relationship, with each one known and loved and cared for.

But the other criterion for building a great church is commitment to the truth; the people in relationship talk – and they talk about things that matter.

Heresies may sound plausible, but truth is what is important (1:4). A man could stand tall and earnest in the pulpit and fix the congregation with Lewis Carroll's poem *Jabberwocky*, recited in a spiritual voice and with a godly smile – but it would still be complete nonsense!

REVIVAL LIVING

> Today we are bombarded by attractive offers, such as: 'By following this simple three-step plan you're guaranteed an inside track.' Don't buy it, says Paul. Don't go there!

People are so gullible. Hardly a month goes by when our newspapers do not highlight some latest heresy about Christianity. Heresy even invades the church. Significant sections of the church are affected, for example, by the belief that if you really have faith you will be rich financially. Or that if you really have faith you will be free from sickness and pain. That is simply not what the Bible teaches.

Paul warns Timothy of the efforts of others to build alternative routes to heavenly places. Today we are bombarded by attractive offers, such as: 'By following this simple three-step plan you're guaranteed an inside track.' Don't buy it, says Paul. Don't go there! Discover God's truth and stick with it. There's a range of options, from the emptiness of the New Age beliefs which sound so spiritual, to the propositional errors of the Jehovah's Witnesses or Mormons or others. As the bedrock of revival we must emphasise commitment to truth.

Recent research from the US questioned people who described themselves as born-again Christians. These were not just churchgoers, but people who claimed to have had the experience of new birth in Jesus. And yet 20 per cent of this group believed in reincarnation, and 26 per cent consulted horoscopes and believed in astrology. Almost half, 45 per cent, believed that 'if people are good enough they can earn a place in heaven'. A quarter of them believed that it could be appropriate to communicate with the dead.

If those figures are even half true, then the level of ignorance among those people who claim to be born-again Bible-believing Christians is frightening. We are committed to truth, and so we should be soaking ourselves in God's Word and living out the truth.

Many people today have fallen for the lie that it's not what you believe that matters, it's what you do. Believe what you want – just act in a kind way. Missionaries have known for centuries that if you find out the kind of god people worship, you will then know about their behaviour. If you have a god who delights in promiscuity, then your behaviour will be promiscuous, and so on. What you believe matters! That is why a church should be bound by conscience, tradition and commitment to emphasise the Bible in its entirety as the foundation for everything. Truth is non-negotiable.

So the church of the third millennium needs a fresh commitment to the truth of Scripture and a turning away from plausible but meaningless alternatives. Christians

the church of the third commitment to the truth of from plausible but

REVIVAL LIVING

need to be weighing whatever they hear about the Christian faith from the pulpit or the newspapers or TV in the light of Scripture. It's not that we should be judgemental, negative and critical. But we need to understand that a lot of what passes for Christianity does not stand the test of analysis.

Imagine you ask me where I went for my holiday and I tell you it was America. You will need to dig below the surface to really know what I mean by 'America'. I may have spent time hiking in the Grand Canyon. Or I may have spent time in the casinos of Las Vegas. Both are in America. But the Grand Canyon and Las Vegas are two totally different worlds. Sometimes we have to search behind whatever big issue is masquerading as Christianity to discover if the detail is really true to the faith.

Not only do we have a responsibility to discover the truth, but Paul says that we have a responsibility to live by it. Truth matters. Behaviour matters. Paul says that the law doesn't worry the innocent, but only the guilty (1:9). It's only when you are breaking the speed limit that it becomes relevant to you. When you are not breaking the law, you don't need to worry about it at all.

One of the characteristics of true revival is conversions. Another is this: when the Holy Spirit comes in power, in genuine revival, there is a significant upgrade in holy living. In other words, behaviour patterns change to be conformed to the will of God. We live in a world where if you are given too much change in a shop and you take it back, people look at you as if you are mad. Standards of integrity and holiness will mark the church out in a world where anything goes, where every year millions of pounds of goods are shoplifted and the prices we pay in the shops have to be inflated to cover those costs.

> It's only when you are breaking the speed limit that it becomes relevant to you. When you are not breaking the law, you don't need to worry about it at all.

So we don't just spout truth about God and what we believe, but the way we live absolutely reeks of morality and integrity and holiness and uprightness. Our word can be trusted. We're squeaky clean, morally. Not that we can believe all the right things and do all the right things without the help of the Holy Spirit – because we are all failed sinners, because the workplace is tough, because family life is difficult. Revival won't come just because we want it to – but because we open ourselves up to the personal refurbishment by the Holy Spirit which we desperately need.

millennium needs a fresh Scripture and a turning away meaningless alternatives

WORKSHEET

Revival Living Worksheet

1: Passing the torch

1 Timothy 1:1–11

1 From this passage, what problems do you think Timothy might have been having in his church?

• Can you draw any parallels in local or national church situations today?

2 Paul's list of lawbreakers in this passage makes for pretty depressing reading, but we could find examples of just the same behaviours in today's newspaper. How do you think Christians can be 'in but not of' the world?

3 How much time and space is there in your church for 'the personal touch'?

• And in your life?

4 Have you ever been sidetracked by myths and endless genealogies (1:4) or meaningless talk (1:6)?

5 How important is truth to you?

• How do you demonstrate your commitment to it?

• How does your church do this?

6 Is your church looking forward to what God will do – or backward to distant moves of the Spirit?

7 Are you passing on or receiving the baton at this point in your life? Or both? Share your experiences on mentoring and being mentored.

8 Pray about any issues that came to light during this discussion.

REVIVAL LIVING

Revival Living
2: Avoiding shipwreck
1 Timothy 1:12–20

Don't be fooled into thinking that if you don't work for one of the big name missionary agencies like Tearfund or YWAM you are not a missionary.

If Monday mornings find you on your way to Rank Xerox or IBM or the RAC or a local government office or a school or a shop, you are just as much sent by God into that setting as are church planters in Indonesia.

Paul says there are three strategic things you need if you are going to be a great servant of God.

The first thing (1:12) is that you are **empowered.** Most of us feel weak and inadequate. We feel like we don't have the strength to do what God calls us to do. We feel a failure. We often feel we have let God down and ourselves down.

Certainly we can't do God's work with just our own energy. For revival living to happen in any church at any time in its history, it will need to be empowered by God. Without that power our service will be perfunctory, very human and very failing because we are weak individuals. Paul, the great apostle, recognised this. He knew that he could not plant churches, he could not preach the gospel and he could not even write incredibly complex and clever theological letters without the power of God in his life. We need the power and fullness of the Holy Spirit. Without that strength and power every day we will be just human agents of enthusiasm – nice, but not enough.

Secondly, Paul says that God considered him **faithful** (1:12). He uses this term eleven times in this letter and it

> We need the power and fullness of the Holy Spirit. Without that strength and power every day we will be just human agents of enthusiasm – nice but not enough

REVIVAL LIVING

> God has no Plan B. He is not going to call on a select army of angels to come and evangelise the world if Plan A fails. Plan A is you and me involved in the missionary task.

means 'trustworthy'. This is amazing, because in Paul's earlier days he had been manifestly untrustworthy. He had failed God spectacularly (1:13). He had plagued the early Church, persecuting the saints, rounding them up and throwing them into prison. So Paul had a great sense of wonder about God considering him trustworthy.

This means that despite my personal failure I can be trusted by God, too. Not because I deserve to be trusted, but because in his grace and mercy he chooses to entrust me with the task of preaching the Good News. God has no Plan B. He is not going to call on a select army of angels to come and evangelise the world if Plan A fails. Plan A is you and me involved in the missionary task.

Thirdly, Paul was **appointed** (1:12). I hope you have prayed about where you are going to spend your life's work. Some are called to work overseas, some in a church, some in a classroom or an office or café kitchen. If you work in the accounts department of your local district council you are as surely engaged in a missionary calling as if God had sent you to Romania or Bangladesh. You are appointed to be wherever you are.

So Paul is **empowered, trustworthy, and appointed**. These are the keys to his success; these will be the keys to the younger Timothy's success; and they are the keys to your success. You might be a failure in your own eyes, but God can empower you, he will trust you and he will appoint you. Paul could easily have boasted that the keys to his success lay in his significant background. He had studied with the élite, he had standing in the Sanhedrin. But he knew that without God he was nothing.

There is nothing so reassuring in life as to know that the power of the Holy Spirit is available to you; that God trusts you even though you have messed up; and that you didn't just arrive where you are by accident but he has appointed you to be where you are.

Have you noticed (1:12,13) how honest Paul is about his past? He does not try to brush it under the carpet and try to impress Timothy with his achievements. He is blunt and

Christ came to save sinners. That's what That's our

REVIVAL LIVING

takes full responsibility for his failings. The disappointments of our past are not hidden from God. Like Paul, we must marvel at the grace of God that can take someone so sinful and turn him or her into someone who can make a significant difference for the kingdom.

One of the troubling aspects of many postmodern people in this early part of the third millennium is that they have no sense of guilt. With no feeling for having done wrong, there is no feeling of need for forgiveness. Our eyes are blinded to the fact of our sin. Our litigation culture promotes an avoidance of personal blame. Everything is always someone else's fault. If you say to someone that he is a sinner, he is offended. It is a very unpopular notion. 'Don't say that, I'm a nice person. I'm kind to people. I give to charity.' Niceness is nothing to do with the gospel. There are a lot of non-Christians who are nicer than Christians.

Since the middle of the last century there has been an escalation in the kind of psychology which passes the buck for all human behaviour. We are told that we behave in certain ways because of our upbringing or our peers or our circumstances. It's not true! Yes, some of us have had traumatic childhoods or difficult pasts, and we shouldn't underestimate the painful effects of that. But the reality is that we need to take responsibility for our own failings. Until we stop blaming everyone else, we'll never know forgiveness.

Admitting our sinfulness is the most releasing experience on the planet. It opens the door for God's grace and mercy to come flooding into our lives. However intelligent, however gifted, however significant we are, however strong our family, we are all in need of God's grace and mercy – and Paul understands this (1:15). Notice that he is not just pointing the finger, because he confesses to being the worst of sinners himself. There is nothing worse than a holier-than-thou posturing in evangelism which condemns people and refuses to share that we too were once lost in our sin.

Wonderfully, this means that there is not a single person who is too bad for God. No sin is so bad that God can't forgive it. On the other hand, there is not a single person who is so nice, so sweet, so cherubic that they are not in desperate need of the grace of God. God can use every single one of us. We have been entrusted with the renewal of our communities and the Good News of Jesus. God still trusts us when we fail; he goes on loving us and pours his grace into our lives.

Paul is so excited here that he goes on to summarise the heart of the gospel (1:15). He begins as if he's introducing a legal document: 'Here is a trustworthy saying…' He does this to flag up that this is pretty serious stuff. It matters. Christ came to save sinners. That's what drives revival living. That's our missionary evangelism mandate.

Notice that Paul describes Jesus as having unlimited patience (1:16). How often do you lose your patience with someone? But then, people are so stupid, aren't they? 'How many times have I told you …?' 'Why didn't you listen the

drives revival living.
missionary evangelism mandate

> In the case of gross moral failure, you are seen to be shipwrecked. The deck is obviously at a precarious angle and awash with water. But there are many gradual shipwrecks where people are holed below the water line, and hardly anyone knows but them.

first time?' We don't have unlimited patience with people because we don't understand all about them and why they do things. But Jesus isn't weak and flawed and limited and he understands exactly why people behave the way they do. Paul says that even when we deserve it, Jesus doesn't write us off, he's patient. And that gets him so excited he launches into a hymn of praise (1:17), the verse which has provided inspiration for the hymn 'Immortal, invisible, God only wise,/ In light inaccessible, hid from our eyes'.

Chapter 1 concludes with two related instructions about not giving up and not rejecting God. One is to go on fighting the good fight (1:18); and the other is to keep the faith and a good conscience (1:19). Paul uses the metaphors of the soldier and the sailor here. Don't give up, he says, in spite of the pressures of the heresies and the struggles in the church. He urges him to hold firm, unlike the two men he mentions, Hymenaeus and Alexander, who have shipwrecked their faith.

One of the enormous pains of pastoral ministry is to talk to people whose lives are heading for the rocks. Sometimes I have had to plead with people because I have seen that the end result of their action is going to be shipwreck; and that's not a reflection on my fantastic insight, because almost any objective observer would draw the same conclusion. Often lives hit the rocks of moral failure. Sometimes it's apparently simple: for example, a one-off sexual indis-

cretion, an aberration that compromises years of faithful Christian living. What a tragedy! At other times there's a gradual drifting from the safe channel towards the rocks of abandoning the faith. Very few people get up one morning and decide that they won't follow Jesus any more. But many people over periods of months and years drift slowly and imperceptibly away from God, almost unnoticed by themselves or others, so that one day it only takes a little nudge to be on the rocks of failure. Over time, it just takes a series of little nudges to draw back from things that are important – like going to church, reading the Bible, sharing your faith. There may be no dramatic sinful downfall, but your love for God grows cold and you end up shipwrecked.

In the case of gross moral failure, you are seen to be shipwrecked. The deck is obviously at a precarious angle and awash with water. But there are many gradual shipwrecks where people are holed below the water line, and hardly anyone knows but them.

So Paul urges Timothy to hold the faith. The shipwrecked life will never enjoy revival living. Revival living is for failures who are pressing on to know God. So round up the failures you know and tell them that God loves them. Tell them there's hope and a future because of the power and the grace of God.

WORKSHEET

Revival Living Worksheet

2: Avoiding shipwreck
1 Timothy 1:12–20

1 When talking about sinners, Paul describes himself as 'the worst (1:15)'. Is he just exaggerating here?

_____

_____

Do you ever feel it's unfair when God saves tyrants or criminals or totally unattractive personalities?

_____

_____

2 Do you have a sense of calling/ appointment in your present role?

_____

_____

• Why/ why not?

_____

_____

3 Can you discover what were the 'prophecies once made' (1:18) about Timothy?

_____

_____

• Why did he need to be reminded about them?

_____

_____

4 Discuss the example of Hymenaeus and Alexander. What do you think Paul means by 'handing them over to Satan'?

_____

_____

• Do you know any other Scripture verses which may be helpful here?

_____

_____

5 How do you feel about the truth that God is longing to find you trustworthy?

_____

_____

• And that he has unlimited patience with you?

_____

_____

6 How can we persuade our postmodern culture that there is a need for individuals to take responsibility for their wrongdoing?

_____

_____

_____

7 Spend some time praying for anyone you fear may be sailing close to the rocks and in danger of shipwreck. Be discrete as to whether you name the people you pray for. And pray for grace for each member of the group, that they may avoid shipwreck.

REVIVAL LIVING

Revival Living
3: Ways to worship
1 Timothy 2:1–15

Public worship is not merely a casual ritual. It is central to all Paul understands of Christian expression.

Yes, Christian living takes place outside the church building. But the hour or so that a Christian family spends together each week is vital. That time equips, blesses, affirms. It involves sharing of each other and sharing of our common vision. We give expression to the reality of our love for one another. Bringing God the best of our lives is something we do together as well as on our own.

Prayer, says Paul (2:1) is a significant feature of corporate worship. Public prayer for people in authority in our nations is crucial. Intercessory prayer engages reality and Spirit. If we never mention in church what's going on in the outside world, it's no wonder that church can seem incredibly irrelevant. God is not just interested in our tiny little world, but in the nations of the world he created. We need to pray for our politicians, for people with clout in the civil service, for the movers and shakers locally, regionally and nationally. Why? For many reasons, not least that we live peaceful lives (2:2). In times of peace the gospel is unhindered.

Paul stresses the priority in worship of telling other people the gospel (2:3–7). We don't exist for our own benefit; we exist firstly for God's benefit and then for the benefit of others. God wants everyone to be saved and to come to know the truth – and that fact should remain centre stage in our public worship.

God, says Paul, sent his Son as a ransom (2:6). Generally, we only use this word in the context of kidnapping. But in Bible times the redemption price or ransom was the price paid to buy a slave back. Every single person was designed to belong to God. But we chose rebellion and sin, turning our backs on God. The death of Jesus on the cross is the ransom price which enables us to be bought back, to be returned from the devil's territory to the kingdom of God.

So, at the heart of public worship, says Paul, there must be evangelistic priority. As we are equipped with the Spirit and refreshed by his power, we are renewed in common vision and purpose to leave the church and live out the mandate of the Scriptures in sharing the gospel.

at the heart of public worship … there must be evangelistic priority

So, what kind of people ought we to be as worshippers? Verses 8 and 9 say the same thing, although one is addressed specifically to men, and the other to women. It's all about living holy lives. In the church in Ephesus, where Timothy was living, there was significant sinfulness. It was an affluent, cosmopolitan city in which materialism and greed were rampant, and sexual impropriety was happening on a massive scale. These things had invaded the church. But Paul points out that they can't be true worshippers unless they are living holy lives.

Paul uses the picture of raised hands (2:8). This Jewish practice symbolises the giving of all of one's life to God. You may have seen photos of Jewish men standing at the Wailing Wall in Jerusalem or praying in the synagogue, rocking backwards and forwards, with their hands raised high. The key is not that the hands are lifted up, but that they are holy. God says that when you come to worship him you must make sure that your hands are clean. Just as at mealtimes we wash our hands before eating, so we wash our hands spiritually before we come to God's table. Our prayer is most effective when we come with clean lives.

He makes the same point about women, but using a different picture. Your dress, he says should not distract from your purpose. In Ephesus, people came to church parading their wealth. Some women would turn up in gorgeous gowns – and Paul is saying that's inappropriate, it's distracting from prayer. And then there's the question of modesty. Many women in Ephesus were sexually provocative. There were huge numbers of prostitutes, including religious temple prostitutes. When they were converted they needed to learn modesty.

Young people today are being greatly influenced by the over-sexualisation of society. It's a frightening trend. It's almost impossible to watch a pop video without being aware of enormously heavy sexual overtones. Our young people are exposed to this continuously, and so it's hardly surprising that sometimes they dress in inappropriate ways. Paul is saying that it is vital that men and women do nothing to distract from worship. Holiness for men and holiness for women is essential to worship God properly. These verses are not an attack on all jewellery or make-

up per se. But our clothing should not distract but reflect a holy lifestyle and sensitivity to each other.

Young people today are being greatly influenced by the over-sexualisation of society

There are two views of the next verses about women (2:11–15), both of which most of us would struggle to accept. The first is that this passage is simply an expression of Paul's culture; in other words, that any man in the first century would have said precisely this. Neither the Jews nor the Greeks believed in women teachers. As a result, the argument goes, we shouldn't take this passage seriously because it was reflecting a particular cultural context. I would challenge that viewpoint, not least because once you say that about this passage you can say it about almost every New Testament doctrine. But if you believe the Bible is the Word of God, that it is vital and significant in the shaping of our lives, then you cannot dismiss any part of it from Genesis to Revelation in a casual way.

The second view is that this passage should simply be taken at face value, that women ought to keep silent and not speak in public at all; they ought never to teach in church nor be in a situation where they exercise any authority where men are somehow beneath them or being led by them in some hierarchical sense.

Some denominations have been very clear that a woman's place is largely in the home and, in the church context, silent. The reason I find this view untenable biblically is because not only do we have to make sense of this passage but we have to make sense of everything the Bible says about men and women in their relationships and about women in their public role. And Paul seems to me to take

REVIVAL LIVING

a different line in other places. In Philippians chapter 4, for example, he talks about Euodia and Syntyche being co-contenders for the gospel, and that certainly does not mean just togetherness as Christians; it seems to mean being together in the apostolic task in some form – preaching or leading or teaching. They were involved in Philippi doing something for God. How could they do it if they were to be completely silent?

Again, there is the fact that Philip had four daughters, all of whom were prophetesses (Acts 21:9). How could they prophesy without speaking? Or maybe they didn't ever do it in church. How could it have worked? There are at least seven women listed in Romans 16 by Paul as people he has appreciated, listing the things they have done. There may well be a woman called Junias in Romans 16:7 who is described as an apostle. And what do we make of Deborah and her role (Judges 4,5)? She had a strategic role in leadership. Or the influence of a woman like Esther? And what about Galatians 3:28: 'There is neither ... male nor female, for you are all one in Christ Jesus'?

It appears to me that the primary thrust of this passage is addressing a situation of enormous complexity in Ephesus. The context is that of widespread worship of the goddess Aphrodite and sexual impropriety, with women priestesses exercising a dominant role in Ephesian culture. Paul is trying to redress the balance, saying that a dominant female culture is not the appropriate culture of the church. He is trying to make sure that all the errors of priestess leadership are not imported into church life.

I believe God wants all men and women to exercise their spiritual gifts. One particular hypocrisy has been the efforts of the church to maintain male leadership in Britain while

> ## the issue in the Garden of Eden is not the apple on the tree but the pair on the ground!

sending single women as missionaries all over the world to plant churches, to preach the gospel and do anything they wanted to do – as long as they were out of sight!

But it also seems to me that there is more than mere local significance to what Paul says here. These are not just principles for the first century. Paul considers men and women to be different and to have different roles. And the Bible does teach that within the context of marriage the man is to be the head of the home (Ephesians 5:22–24). It seems to me that the Bible teaches this as a permanent and eternally relevant paradigm for marriage. Not that male leadership or headship should be manipulative or vicious or overbearing but that it is present.

Secondly, although I struggle with this view, the emphasis of Scripture suggests to me that the ultimate authority in a local church ought to be male. My personal understanding of the biblical principles is that it should be men who regularly expound the Scriptures to the church, even though there may well be many opportunities for women to teach and preach, under the corporate headship. (I have

> ## One particular hypocrisy has been male leadership in Britain while all over the world to plant churches, anything they wanted to do –

REVIVAL LIVING

championed the releasing of women in the church into ministry and two decades ago my views would have been seen as quite liberal. But there has been such a massive swing in evangelicalism in our times over the role of women that I am aware that today my views may seem narrow to many.)

Fundamentally, however, the thrust of Paul's teaching here is that public worship should never be dominated in a manipulative way by any man or woman, but that we should all come with holy hands lifted up in worship and praise to God.

Paul goes on (2:13,14) to state the facts from the Genesis account. Eve took the fruit, having been deceived by the serpent, and then encouraged her husband into that betrayal. They are both equally culpable. As I often say, the issue in the Garden of Eden is not the apple on the tree but the pair on the ground! Adam and Eve are flawed individuals who rebelled against God.

What is Paul saying in verse 15 about women being saved through childbearing? The original language is very complex. Commentators have suggested that it means that women will be kept safe through the process of giving birth to babies. It seems to me that that is completely out of keeping with the context of this passage. There is no reason why Paul would suddenly talk about the birth process here. I think it is to do, again, with the context of a permissive and badly-run society in Ephesus. The many prostitutes in Ephesus were nicknamed 'bees' because they went from man to man as bees go from flower to flower taking the pollen, taking the men's seeds. The fear was that in this woman-dominated society the male leadership in the church would be usurped by women with immoral intents.

I think Paul is telling Timothy that actually the role of child-bearing, and by implication the role of quietly raising a family, is not without honour. Some of these women needed saving from a life of sensuality and usurping authority to settle down and be part of a family. To add more weight to this, you can compare this passage with Paul's instructions to younger widows in 5:11–15. All this is not to say that every woman needs children; it is not to say that every woman should be married. Paul is making a general point that loving a husband, raising children and nurturing a family is an honourable and significant task for a woman to fulfil.

Paul was addressing a particular imbalance in Ephesian society. As we address our culture in the context of women's liberation, we need to assert that the wife who stays at home and raises children is not somehow inferior to the woman who seeks out a career. Conversely, the message for single women or married women who have not had children is that their state is also a perfectly valid expression of their faith.

the efforts of the church to maintain sending single women as missionaries to preach the gospel and do as long as they were out of sight!

WORKSHEET

Revival Living Worksheet

3: Ways to worship
1 Timothy 2:1–15

1 Why, according to Paul in these verses, is prayer so important?

2 We live in days when many political leaders have been seen to be less than pure. How is it possible to honestly pray for all those in authority?

3 Are there excesses in our society which have invaded worship times in the church?

4 Is lack of modesty an issue in your church?

- How can it be sensitively addressed?

5 In what ways have you benefited from the ministry or gifting of women? Share your experiences.

6 Do you agree with Stephen Gaukroger's interpretation of the second half of this passage in reference to the ministry of Christian women? (Please remember to disagree in love!)

7 Pray for godly men and women to be recognised and raised up in effective leadership both locally and nationally.

REVIVAL LIVING

Revival Living
4: Character for leaders
1 Timothy 3:1–13; 4:9–16

Leadership is a hot potato issue in our society. It's a subject looking for a focus.

Many in the business world admit that they are struggling to find models of excellence in leadership that really work, especially with an increasingly articulate and intelligent workforce. What paradigms of leadership motivate people? Is it strong masculine leadership? Is it something softer?

What about the quality of Christian leaders? Hardly a week goes by without leadership in the church getting into trouble. A Christian leader needs to be clear that his priority is not programmes and structures but the living God. Anything which replaces the living God as my hope is an idol and will lead me ultimately into wrong paths both in my Christian life and in terms of leadership. These fundamentals need to be reawakened in our souls from time to time.

When the Bible makes demands on its leaders, it is presenting paradigms for the whole people of God. So, whether or not you are a leader, Paul's teaching to Timothy on godly leadership holds true. If we want to live in revival as a church, there will be particular demands on anyone who aspires to any form of leadership to live according to the characteristics Paul describes here. This applies equally to someone leading a church home group or serving a local church as a deacon as to someone leading a section of their

office or a factory department or college or to someone working with children or young people. Christian leadership is Christian leadership wherever it is exercised.

Paul tells us here that Christian leadership is both plural and moral. It's plural because there's safety within working in teams. That's surprising, because most leadership in the Bible is singular. We can easily think of examples: Moses, David, Joshua, Jesus. But these are notable exceptions. Yes, there is a place for visionary individual leadership – but the Bible says it's generally not safe. A leader needs to be surrounded by a support system, an accountability struc-

> A Christian leader needs to be clear that his priority is not programmes and structures but the living God

ture. A team setting makes leadership flourish. We all have different natural and spiritual gifting, and a leader needs to be complemented by others.

This passage is not so much about skills in leadership but as about excellence in character. Many Christian leaders founder on the rock of ungodly character. Charisma and gifting without character have no credibility.

It's worth remembering that the various terms such as bishops, overseers, deacons and elders are all interchangeable and overlapping – there is no standard structure of leadership in the New Testament. There are principles, but no set pattern. However, the term translated as 'the wives' in the NIV (3:11) may well mean deaconesses, or women exercising leadership roles rather than the wives of the leaders. In these early days it was generally the wives of leaders who were the women leaders. Sadly, this verse is one that has encouraged the church to be incredibly patronising to women in leadership, which is unforgivable.

Overall, this passage is very challenging for all leaders. There is all the difference in the world between teaching truth and actually owning it deep inside. Godly character flows from a heart which has been transformed by the truth you teach. It is like the difference between a teacher mugging up the next page in the book in order to teach the class the next day and a teacher who has an incredible love for the subject and knows it inside out and backwards.

It is fascinating that at the outset of this passage (3:1)

Charisma and gifting without character have no credibility.

Paul affirms godly ambition. We have often scoffed at ambition in the church. We've associated it with pride. But Paul seems to be saying 'Well done' to those who aspire for the right motives to take on leadership roles, particularly in the church, to lead the people of God forward. Godly ambition means wanting to be more than we are, for the sake of the kingdom. Scripture frowns on ambition which is selfish, status-seeking, self-aggrandising. Some people are intoxicated by the power of leadership, or the apparent influence it brings. Many want to be a leader for the status, to be the focus of attention, but very few want the demands of heavy workload, commitment and vulnerability to the public gaze.

The main character requirement is to be above reproach (3:2). Paul goes on to define what he means by this. In an Ephesian world of polygamy, prostitution and sexual excess, Paul says a leader must be self-controlled and above reproach sexually. He must be even in terms of temper, attitude and emotion. An open hand, an open heart and an open home are also desirable characteristics of leadership.

Some people are intoxicated or the apparent influence it brings. a leader for the status, but very few want the demands

REVIVAL LIVING

The leader must be able to pass on the faith to others. He must be able to handle alcohol (3:3) – not that alcohol is more of a problem than other issues such as pride – but it's one area that demonstrates a life out of balance. Paul says a leader must not be violent but gentle, not quarrelsome, not a lover of money.

Character is important. There have been many occasions when I have been either directly involved in counselling or I have got to hear about national leaders or church leaders who have committed adultery or stolen from their church. There is enormous pressure on Christian leadership today. That's why a church leadership team needs to set guidelines about such things as leaders spending time with their families and not counselling members of the opposite sex. Without those guidelines we are vulnerable to temptation or to accusation which may be unfounded. For example, although I am the senior pastor of a church, I am not able to sign cheques, which I find enormously releasing. There's no way I can help myself from the church budget. Neither do I know which church members give money and how much. When a church leader falls into temptation in these areas, Satan is thrilled and the kingdom is damaged.

Recently I was hearing about a couple of Oxford students who were producing GCSE and A-level essays on the Internet for secondary pupils to download. Their website gave advice on how students could tinker with them slightly so that the essays will look their own. By changing a few words and even popping in a few deliberate errors, you can pass off one of the essays as your own. One of the people behind it said that if you didn't get caught it was fine. There's an interesting moral framework here, that this is only wrong if you get caught. This particular moral framework affects most of our country and is applied to many issues: it's wrong if you get caught but OK if you get away with it. The Christian moral ethic is actually the opposite: it's wrong whether or not you get caught! Getting caught is irrelevant to God. Your heart should be above reproach.

Paul says that in order to manage God's family well, a leader must manage his own (3:4). If you have children who behave appallingly and believe this excludes you from leadership it will be helpful to know that there does reach a point – in Jewish terms it would be around the age of 12 or 13 – when our children take responsibility for their own lives and we cease to bear primary responsibility for the way they act. Undoubtedly people who do not care for their own family appropriately ought not to put themselves forward for church leadership, because they need to be investing time in the family and making that a priority. But when children are grown, even if they have gone off the rails spiritually, you are not disqualified from serving as a leader.

As to maturity, Paul says a leader must not be a recent convert (3:6), because pride will inevitably be the result of a fast-track elevation. Be careful to give people time to grow in their faith. A good reputation is important (3:7), not just within but outside the church. Someone who is known in business as sailing very close to the wind in terms of their ethical dealings, or known for their sharp practices in the

by the power of leadership, Many want to be to be the focus of attention, of heavy workload, commitment and vulnerability to the public gaze

> We're not looking at the end of life to the morphine-induced haze which sees us pass painlessly through the jaws of death, nor to the ventilator which keeps us alive for a few days longer. No, we look to Jesus and his risen power. What a sad bunch we are if Jesus is not alive!

world, however they behave in the church, needs to be disqualified from oversight in the church. There must be integrity and consistency.

Paul advises that there must be testing for higher leadership (3:10) to ensure that the call is clear, that character is genuine, that there is real humility. When we live this way, revival living for us and the church becomes a real possibility.

Paul says that a good leader is always focused on Christian hope (4:10). Our God is alive. He transcends death. We're not looking at the end of life to the morphine-induced haze which sees us pass painlessly through the jaws of death, nor to the ventilator which keeps us alive for a few days longer. No, we look to Jesus and his risen power. What a sad bunch we are if Jesus is not alive! Paul tells Timothy he'll be a leader worth something if his hope is fixed on the living God.

Paul also commends Timothy to be authoritative, in command (4:11). This is not a very politically correct idea. But Paul says good church leaders are not wishy-washy about the truth but teach it with authority. Don't be authoritarian and controlling, but assert the authority of the Bible. Leaders should keep Scripture central (4:13). Are you addicted to the Bible? Obsessed with it? Devoted to it? Feeding on it in public and in private?

Timothy was youthful, probably under 40, and that was

difficult in the first century because in Jewish culture old age was venerated. But Paul says he shouldn't let people patronise him (4:12). His defence for anyone who criticises his youth will be his godly lifestyle. The testimony of our lives will shout the loudest and silence would-be critics.

Timothy had been commissioned for service and Paul says he must not neglect his gifting, otherwise it risks decay (4:14). We can sacrifice our gifts to a crowded and stressful lifestyle, squeezed out until they are no longer operating.

An effective leader is whole-hearted (4:15). There's a danger in becoming so comfortable with our skills that we perform in a perfunctory or routine way. You can go through the motions of running a home group, for example. You can lose your passion in preaching. We must keep our faith fresh and our leadership passionate.

Finally, a good leader knows that his life must mirror his doctrine (4:16). We must persevere at getting that consistently right, even when we feel like giving up because it seems we're not getting anywhere. We must constantly seek the Holy Spirit to breathe over us and fan into life the embers of our faith to make a roaring flame.

WORKSHEET

Revival Living Worksheet

4: Character for leaders

1 Timothy 3:1–13; 4:9–16

1 Is there a good structure of teamwork and accountability in your church leadership?

- Are there things that need improving?

- Areas of vulnerability?

2 How can we identify whether ambition is godly or self-seeking?

3 Why is the home such an important place for the Christian, and so often such a difficult place to be one?

4 It's possible that Timothy's leadership had been called into question because of his relatively young age (4:12). Have you ever been patronised in the church for your youth? Your gender? Your social background? How can the church tackle this?

5 Why do we need to be diligent (4:15) and persevere (4:16)? What's wrong with simply relying on the Holy Spirit to empower and enable us?

6 What strategies can be adopted in a local church to identify and nurture the gifts of men and women equally?

7 Spend some time praying for elders and deacons or other kinds of church officers and their families.

REVIVAL LIVING

Revival Living
5: Living in the truth
1 Timothy 3:14-16

There is a vital relationship between understanding truth and behaving in the light of that understanding.

Suppose you are learning to drive a car and when you pull away from the kerb the car leaps like a kangaroo. That's a frustrating experience. But suppose your driving instructor says, 'Wait a minute. I don't think you've got the first clue about what's going on under the bonnet. Let me explain. That clutch pedal on the floor disengages the engine from the wheels. So when you put the clutch down, the car stops going forwards. The engine will not propel you forwards any more. When you bring it back up, then the engine will engage the wheels and drive you forward. That's why when you take your foot off the clutch too suddenly you go err-rump.' Hopefully, understanding a bit of how everything connects under the bonnet means that you behave differently.

That's exactly what Paul wants. He wants Timothy to understand the connection between truth and behaviour, and to teach it in the church. He wants this not just for the truth's sake, but because understanding the truth has the power to set people free and enable them to live as they were created to live.

If you think the church is merely a building, then for six days a week it will be remote from you. If church for you is a kind of theatre, then you will live and behave as though you are a kind of spectator. But Paul says the church isn't like that (3:15). The church is the possession of the living God. The church is inextricably bound up with the living Jesus.

Paul uses four words (3:15) that are fundamentally important for our understanding of the church and the way we should behave.

First of all, **the church is a household.** The church is not something you go to, it is something you belong to. It is people, not a building. It is a household, a brotherhood and

> understanding the truth has the power to set people free and enable them to live as they were created to live

REVIVAL LIVING

sisterhood, brought together by the fatherhood of God. The household needs to be committed to love one another.

And then he says **the church is an assembly**. The word for church is *ecclesia*, which means it is made up of people

is to live a victorious life in the classroom, in college, in the home, in the office, in the hospital? How can we live lives that are not just like everyone else's outside the church – but lives that are absolutely different? How can we dare to be different?

How can we live lives that are not just like everyone else's outside the church – but lives that are absolutely different? How can we dare to be different?

who have been 'called out'. In the first century world the town crier would call citizens out from their homes for an important announcement. This gathering was called an *ecclesia*: those who have been called out. Paul uses the same word to describe the church. The church is made up of those who have been called out – called out to Jesus, called out into a relationship, called out from darkness into light.

Also, **the church is a pillar**. In Ephesus there was a temple right in the middle of the city, dedicated to Artemis or Diana. And in that temple there were something like 127 pillars – beautiful pillars, not just chunks of rock but fabulously decorated. Some were overlaid with gold, encrusted with precious stones. Paul is saying here that the church is a lovely pillar of the truth. The church needs to display the truth. 'Timothy, do you think the Temple of Artemis is beautiful? Spectacular? That's not a patch on the truth of Almighty God,' says Paul. The church needs to display the wonderful truth of God.

And finally, Paul says **the church is the foundation of truth**. The church must be the community where the truth is loved, owned, proclaimed and lived out – where the truth of the gospel matters supremely and governs all of life.

Then Paul goes on to a vital question (3:16). How can people live godly lives? How can you and I know what it

Paul says that the answer is really all about Jesus. If you have a wrong view of who Jesus is and why he came and what he did; if for you he is rotting in some tomb in Galilee; then that is going to impact the kind of life you live and the kind of hope you have. Your view of your future destiny will be dramatically affected.

Paul asserts that Jesus was a real human being (3:16). Not everyone understood that then and not everyone understands that now. For example, one sect around at this time, the Donatists, believed that Jesus was so godlike that he wasn't really human at all. They believed that if he walked along the beach he would not leave any footprints. But the Bible asserts that Jesus was fully human. 'In the beginning was the Word' (John 1:1). 'The Word became flesh' (John 1:14). When he came into our lost world Jesus needed to know what it was really like to be human. Jesus knows what it is to struggle from Monday through to Friday.

Next, we read that Jesus was 'vindicated by the Spirit' (3:16). The whole ministry of Jesus was characterised by dependence on the Holy Spirit. We see again and again the Spirit of God coming down upon Jesus: at his baptism, in his temptations, in his ministry. The Holy Spirit came upon him and empowered him to live the life. Jesus did not have any magical monopoly on the Holy Spirit. You and I need to experience the empowering of the Holy Spirit and to

I meet Christians who are broken and defeated because they have stopped holding the truth and have started believing their own feelings or their own perceptions regarding the truth

know that it is possible to live a godly life because of Jesus and the Holy Spirit.

Jesus was 'seen by angels'(3:16). This has perplexed quite a few scholars. It could be a reference to Jesus in his pre-incarnate form before he became a human being. Or it could mean his life on earth with the whole heavenly host watching and witnessing.

Jesus was 'preached among the nations'(3:16). It's incredible but true, that something between 75,000 and 110,000 people put their trust in Jesus every single day. Jesus in Matthew 28:19,20 gave the church its marching orders: '... go and make disciples of all nations, baptising them in the name of the Father and of the Son and of the Holy Spirit, and teaching them to obey everything I have commanded you'. He has never ever renounced that commission. People everywhere are believing in Jesus – this Jesus who blazed a trail for us into heaven so that we could follow.

God is interested in your world. He knows your world and wants to be a part of it with you. He sent Jesus Christ to die on the cross that you might be forgiven and go to heaven. Jesus sent us his Spirit, the same Spirit who empowered him and enabled him to live for God according to his word who can energise our lives to live for Jesus as a part of his church.

I meet Christians who are broken and defeated because they have stopped holding the truth and have started believing their own feelings or their own perceptions regarding the truth. I often give them a whole list of

wonderful truths about Jesus I've taken from Neil Anderson's excellent book, *Victory over the Darkness*. Here are just a few of those truths.

Why should I say I can't when the Bible says I can do everything through him who gives me strength? Philippians 4:13.

Why should I feel afraid, when the Bible says God did not give us a spirit of timidity, but a spirit of power, of love and of self-discipline? 2 Timothy 1:7.

Why should I allow Satan to have control over my life and my destiny when the Bible says the one who is in you is greater than the one who is in the world? 1 John 4:4.

Why should I worry and be upset and dominated when I can cast all my anxiety on Christ, who cares for me? 1 Peter 5:7.

Why should I feel alone when Jesus said he is with me always, and will never leave me nor forsake me? Matthew 28:20; Hebrews 13:5.

Why should I feel like a failure when I am a conqueror in all things, through Christ who loves me? Romans 8:37.

Knowing these truths can dramatically affect your life, your behaviour, your character, as you allow the Holy Spirit to take the living Word and apply it.

WORKSHEET

Revival Living Worksheet

5: Living in the truth

1 Timothy 3:14–16

1 In what ways is your church functioning as a household or family?

_____

_____

• Can you think of ways to develop this?

_____

_____

2 What impact on behaviour might result from grasping the truth about
• the humanity of Jesus?

_____

_____

• the divinity of Jesus?

_____

_____

• the dependence of Jesus on the Holy Spirit?

_____

_____

• the commission Jesus left his followers (Matthew 28:16–20)?

_____

_____

3 Spend some time on your own re-reading the checklist of truths on the previous page.

_____

_____

• Which is most relevant to your current situation?

_____

_____

4 Share in the group and pray for one another.

REVIVAL LIVING

Revival Living
6: Fit and free

1 Timothy 4:1–8

False teaching is not something from another time and place – it's widespread in our western societies.

You frequently open a national newspaper and find a centre page spread in which so-called experts are interviewed to tell you that a certain part of the Bible has been discredited, or a certain theologian has come up with a novel view of Jesus which is quite non-biblical. Or there is a story suggesting that somewhere hidden in the pages of the New Testament is a sort of computer-generated code which will somehow unpack some new teaching.

There is always something new to colour the way people think about Christianity. There is an incredible proliferation of cults and sects, many of which look very plausible. They use the Bible, they use the name of Jesus. It sounds like Christianity but in fact, on closer examination, it's just a little road that for a while runs parallel with Christianity and then, almost imperceptibly, heads off in an entirely different direction.

From looking at embracing Jesus and his truth so that it impacts our lives, we move in chapter 4 into Paul's warning to Timothy to distance himself from ungodliness and false teaching.

Paul, often so gracious and measured, uses plenty of emotional energy and venom in describing those responsible for false teaching. 'Hypocritical liars', he calls them (4:2). He sees the fledgling church in Ephesus and the young Timothy trying to cope. A torrent of false teaching threatens to engulf the church in a kind of tidal wave and, Canute-like, Timothy is trying to hold it back. Paul is livid that his precious spiritual children are in danger of being corrupted by this false teaching.

What is it that protects you from false teaching and heresy? Or perhaps you believe you are completely immune from believing the wrong things about God? One key to the corrective process is being in fellowship with one another. Those who neglect the body of Christ are particularly in danger of having their spiritual compass corrupted.

> What is it that protects you from false teaching and heresy?

REVIVAL LIVING

Christians frequently fall into the trap of a dualistic view of life, where religious life is kept in one box

Abandonment of the truth for some erroneous doctrine is rarely a willful, dramatic action. More commonly, it happens without people realising it. Some people may be outwardly behaving as believers, while mentally they have been progressively abandoning belief over a period of months or years.

The origin of false teaching is demonic. Fortunately the early church had a healthy understanding that what they could see and touch wasn't all there was. They understood about real but invisible demonic powers. Today, when we think about the demonic we think of spectacular special effects from *The Exorcist*. Though Satan does sometimes operate in dramatic ways, his main activities are more subtle. He operates in the arenas of political and corporate corruption, deceptions and distortions on a grand scale or minor indiscretions on the personal level. Or he's at work blinding people. Have you ever wondered why people cannot seem to see the truths of Christianity? They are blind! They can't respond to the gospel, not because the witnessing isn't persuasive enough, but because they are blinded by Satan. The only thing that will remove the veil is the power of the Holy Spirit.

Paul says false teaching is demonically inspired but has human agency. It comes through 'hypocritical liars, whose consciences have been seared as with a hot iron' (4:2). If you burn your hand badly it becomes insensitive for a while. Only with healing does sensation come back. These false teachers are so seared that their nerve endings are insensitive to God. They are unknowing agents of the devil.

As illustration Paul says, 'they forbid people to marry and they order them to abstain from certain kinds of food'. Many heretical groups treated the human body and natural appetites as if they were worldly and sinful, and this idea is still around 2000 years later. Whenever people enjoy a really good meal, they instinctively feel sinful because they have been satisfying the lust of the flesh, their appetite. It is part of our puritanical background to believe that if we are enjoying ourselves we must be sinning. Even some of

the early church fathers believed that somehow being a virgin was more acceptable to God than someone who was married. Now, this is not a biblical view of life, but the bondage of false teaching. The Bible says that actually all things are created by God for us to enjoy and be thankful for, within godly frameworks. So, for example, the framework within which sexuality is to be enjoyed is that of marriage.

Christians frequently fall into the trap of a dualistic view of life, where religious life is kept in one box and other kinds of life – at work, in the home, on the sports field and so on – in another box. But God wants everything to be in the 'Christian life' box, so that Jesus permeates everything.

I frequently talk with people whose lives appear to be models of faith in terms of church attendance, Bible reading and prayer. And then I discover that they have been having a secret adulterous affair for a number of years or have been involved in an illegal business deal. These people contain their sins with calm equanimity because they live their lives in separate boxes.

How do we live with our faith affecting all parts of our life? Just as keeping the body fit is tough discipline, so is living a consistently godly life. It's a struggle sometimes to read the Bible. So, says Paul, get into God's gymnasium. One discipline is to make ourselves accountable to others, whether that's a prayer triplet or a small group. Find someone you can relate to who will help you stay honest about your spiritual disciplines, who will help you fight the spiritual flab and strengthen the spiritual muscles. The challenge is to maintain spiritual fitness and not to become ineffective spiritually, with a weak prayer life, a loss of enthusiasm for evangelism, a lack of interest in the Bible, and a disinclination to worship. We want to be fit to serve God, fit to share our faith, fit to follow Jesus and love him day by day.

WORKSHEET

Revival Living Worksheet

6: Fit and free
1 Timothy 4:1–8

1 G K Chesterton (critic, novelist and poet 1874–1936) says about this passage and about sanctifying all we do: 'You say grace before meals. All right. But I say grace before the play and the opera and grace before the concert and pantomime and grace before I open a book and grace before sketching and painting and grace before swimming and fencing and boxing and walking and playing and dancing and grace before I dip the pen in the ink.' How can we avoid compartmentalising our faith, and so live the whole of our lives with an awareness of God?

_____

_____

_____

2 To what extent have you encountered false legalism and other false teaching?

_____

_____

- What protection from false teaching is there in your life?

_____

_____

- How can we achieve a good balance between legalism and an 'anything goes' attitude?

_____

_____

3 What do you think of Stephen Gaukroger's comments on why some people cannot see the truths of the gospel?

_____

_____

- How might this change our attitude to evangelism?

_____

_____

- And our prayer for non-Christians?

_____

_____

_____

4 Spend some time praying as a group for the godliness of 4:8 to be demonstrated in your lives and the witness of your church.

REVIVAL LIVING

Revival Living
7: Family love
1 Timothy 5:1–16

Our newspapers are filled with stories of elderly people, often women living alone, being brutally bludgeoned to death, sometimes raped in horrific circumstances. Age is despised and ridiculed.

Our tendency as a society is to put our old people as far away from attention as possible. In contrast, the Bible affords all men and women a place of dignity, and encourages us to treat them accordingly.

Central in this passage is 5:8. Paul says you can pontificate all you want about your beliefs, but unless it results in actions you are a hypocrite. Overall the passage gives excellent advice for anyone in any kind of leadership in the church as to how to deal with all kinds of people. For example, you should not treat older men and women harshly but with respect. Now that is very anti-cultural in a western society that's youth-dominated.

Old age, of course, is a state of mind as well as a chronology of years. If you had lived to 60 in those days you deserved to be cared for by the church, whereas today people are living so much longer that 60 is almost still in the category of middle-aged.

As for your peers, Paul advises Timothy, treat them as brothers and sisters (5:1,2). That rules out a sexually predatory attitude in the life of the church. We can be sound as

a bell theologically but Paul says it counts for little if our relationships aren't pure. We have to be warm and affectionate to each other but without the slightest tinge of sexual exploitation. We need to model strong same-sex relationship without a hint of homosexual implications.

The society of the early church included people who were marginalised from support and love, many of them widows. That's the true nature of church. It helps those on the edge, who fall through the safety nets, who fall through the cracks. Widows in Timothy's time exemplified the most vulnerable in society. There was no provision for them. Paul tells Timothy that the church must care for the vulnerable. Christianity is not about a list of facts we believe, but about a faith that deeply impacts our relationships, particularly with the marginalised, the poor, the needy, the struggling. This whole section sets out Paul's strong view on social compassion.

To our ears, some of these verses sound chauvinistic and paternalistic. For example, 5:14,15 might be interpreted as saying that poor young widows should go and find husbands and have babies and all their problems will be solved! No one would dream of saying such a thing today! But in first-century culture this was practical and helpful advice. There were very few other opportunities for support and care. Don't forget that life expectancy rates were much lower, so it was possible to be quite alone and unsupported in your forties. Your first line of care was your own children and grandchildren, but if you had none then the responsibility rested with the church. But even then, Paul says, the widows needed to be behaving properly (5:13). They shouldn't be idle, but actively involved in acts of kindness and hospitality.

The church must act wisely and lovingly towards those in need but not waste its time caring for people who could be cared for by others. The church must focus on those who have no one to give them love. We are family. If someone has a family of unbelievers, even if we do not need to give them physical care, they need spiritual family support from us.

'See how these Christians love one another,' wrote Tertullian. The love validates the truth. When the poor, the sad, and the struggling know the church is a place where

The church must focus on those who have no one to give them love. We are family

Jesus, of course, often ministered to widows. The widow of Nain was the mother of a son who had died. Jesus raised him from the dead (Luke 7:11–15). People think it was simply a great miracle of healing. Actually, it was also a great economic miracle. Jesus was protecting the widow from starving to death. If he had not raised the child she would never have been fed. Jesus was both showing compassion to the woman and providing for her future.

Jesus pointed to widows as examples of godliness. Do you remember the example of the rich guys making a show of their offering in the Temple, and the widow with her two pennies which she threw in, almost embarrassed (Mark 12:41–44)? She was an example of godliness. So this is not a one-way street. Being supportive to the vulnerable may well prove a blessing to the church in providing godly role models. But even if not, James wrote about true religion as helping the fatherless and the widows (James 1:27).

So when you read 'widows' here, don't just think of widows. It is important to care for anybody who is alone, isolated or vulnerable.

they are loved and treasured and have their needs met, then Jesus is honoured and others will be drawn to the church to discover the secret of this love.

WORKSHEET

Revival Living Worksheet

7: Family love
1 Timothy 5:1–16

1   In our days we have a culture of professional care for the elderly, sick and needy, with hospices, nursing homes, psychiatric units and so on. So is the teaching in 5:8 now redundant?

_____

_____

_____

2   If you were writing a charter for caring for your local church, who would you identify as your 'widows' – the vulnerable people in your community?

_____

_____

•   What kinds of caring are most appropriate for these groups? Financial? Practical? Friendship?

_____

_____

•   Is your church making a response?

_____

_____

3   How can we preserve the right balance between providing for both the practical and spiritual needs of the needy?

_____

_____

•   Are you aware of Christian programmes that have failed to maintain this balance? And some that have succeeded?

_____

_____

4   Discuss James 1:27. How do you explain the link James implies between caring for the needy and keeping yourself 'from being polluted by the world'?

_____

_____

_____

5   What is your church known for?

_____

_____

•   Does it have a reputation for love?

_____

_____

REVIVAL LIVING

Revival Living
8: More leadership advice
1 Timothy 5:17–25

When we think of revival we think of thousands of people running into the kingdom of God.

We imagine people from all sectors of society transformed by the power of the living God. We think of prisons being emptied. We see politics and business and the arts and the media transformed by the Good News. We picture churches bulging at the seams with people desperate to find out about God. We think of the weeping that accompanies deep repentance that is a sign of true revival.

Yes, that is revival – and hardly a genuine Christian anywhere does not pray for that kind of revival. But revival also happens at the micro level, the small you-and-me level. Revival is for people with worries about their health or their weight or their bank balance or their children or their parents. It touches the ordinary and the mundane as well as the big picture of the nations.

If we only think of the big picture of revival it's tempting to pray for that big move of God but miss the fact that revival is about you and me sitting under the authority of the Bible, living our lives in obedience to the Word.

Paul says that those who preach and teach are worthy of double honour (5:17). There is some evidence that the early church fathers interpreted that as meaning they should be paid double! But, sadly for me as a preacher, I'm not quite sure this was what Paul had in mind! Certainly Christian workers should be paid appropriately. Paul quotes Jesus, who said that a worker deserves proper pay (Luke 10:7).

> most of us have a predisposition to believe bad news. We love a conspiracy theory!

REVIVAL LIVING

But the word honour means more than payment. It refers to respect. This is because what is being preached is God's Word, which is worthy of respect. It is no ordinary book. Churches and missionary organisations that treat their employees in a cavalier way will come under the judgement of God.

However, how to interpret this verse properly is not easy. Double what? Paul talks about the leadership exercising accountability and our need to be loyal to our leaders, although that should not be blind loyalty. He explains the principle of making sure any accusation against a minister is true by confirming it from others (5:19).

God'. Stern words. If we have something against another person we need to have it out with that person in a way which is honourable. Far too many decisions in church life are formed on the basis of either complete untruths or half truths.

Wrong perceptions can quickly seem like truth. Suppose I tell my congregation that petrol deliveries throughout the county are to be stopped at midnight for a week. It would be a complete lie. But if everyone believes me, and lets all their friends and families know, it becomes a self-fulfilling prophecy as everyone rushes out to fill up their tanks and actually causes a petrol shortage.

gossip and conjecture in the life of the church can easily become a self-fulfilling prophecy. People are quite capable of creating their own realities

It's quite likely that the young Timothy was the victim of hate mail and criticism. How should he deal with that? How should today's young pastors deal with it? Unfortunately, most of us have a predisposition to believe bad news. We love a conspiracy theory! No one in leadership is immune from destructive criticism and wrong accusation. Close communities always generate gossip. Paul says that that kind of accusation should not be allowed. Deal with private accusations in private, in confidence, he advises. And where such criticisms come into the public arena, they should be dealt with publicly.

A well-known Scottish pastor writing over 50 years ago said: 'This permanent fact remains: that this would be a happier world, and the church too would be happier, if people would realise that it is nothing less than sin to spread stories of whose truth they are not sure. Irresponsible, slanderous and malicious talk does infinite damage and causes infinite heartbreak and such talk will not go unpunished by

Similarly, gossip and conjecture in the life of the church can easily become a self-fulfilling prophecy. People are quite capable of creating their own realities. That's exactly what was happening to the church in Ephesus.

In verse 21, Paul puts his finger on a key struggle for every pastor and every leader – the need to avoid favouritism. Pastors are only human and they live with the temptation to give a better pastoral service to the rich, the attractive, the warm, the encouraging.

Imagine I lead a home group. There are one or two members I really like because they contribute well and they say I'm a great leader. But there are others who don't come very regularly, and when they do they are a pain in the neck. God calls me to care for all the group members without favouritism. The pressure is to be really nice to those who are nice to us. But leaders have to bend over backwards to avoid partiality.

The next advice from Paul is not to be hasty in appointing people for ministry (5:22). Most immature Christians will crack under pressure and they won't be able to avoid favouritism. Leadership is tremendously challenging, demanding maturity.

Next, Paul goes on to suggest that Timothy isn't really looking after himself (5:23). Some leaders tend to be workaholics and ignore their health. Perhaps Timothy had a puritanical kind of view, avoiding alcohol, and Paul,

All of us in leadership need to take care of ourselves – body, mind and spirit. We have a responsibility to do so.

Finally in this section, Paul talks about appearances and how deceptive they can be. And he uses this very odd little phrase: 'The sins of some men are obvious'. They reach the place of judgement ahead of them; and other people have sins which trail behind them (5:24). Some people's sinful reputations run ahead of them. So if I mention Adolf Hitler or Idi Amin, quite likely you will know little about

The leader of excellence has an authentic spirituality that goes deeper than the superficial and fully demonstrates a life given over to God

concerned about the younger man's health, says, 'Medicinally, I think it would be better if you drank some wine from time to time to settle your stomach.' Let's not forget that in the first century the water was often quite dangerous to drink!

Personally, I practise total abstinence. But I don't do it from a belief that the Bible teaches total abstinence. I have had friends who did believe the Bible taught that, and when they came to this verse they did not know what to make of it apart from saying that maybe Paul assumed the wine was to be applied externally! Well, that's obviously nonsense. Paul intended Timothy to drink it. And indeed Jesus drank alcohol, including the wine of the Last Supper celebration. Wine was much more common in the ancient world. Today the medicinal value of a little red wine is recognised – and notice that Paul uses the word 'little' here.

But any leader who abuses alcohol ought not to be in Christian leadership. Alcoholism is a horrendous social disease. Though the Bible does not call anyone to abstinence, I believe the Holy Spirit calls me personally to abstinence.

their personal lives but something more about their deeds of grotesque butchery. Their awful reputations are paramount. They are easy to spot. But there are others, Paul says, whose evil deeds trail behind them. They are also dangerous. Everything looks fine on the surface – but wait awhile and you will see evil results from their life and behaviour. The leader of excellence has an authentic spirituality that goes deeper than the superficial and fully demonstrates a life given over to God.

WORKSHEET

Revival Living Worksheet

8: More leadership advice
1 Timothy 5:17–25

1 Do you find it easier to recognise the hand of God in the big dramatic events on the world stage, or in the minutiae of the daily lives of individuals?

_____

_____

_____

2 Is it reasonable/ desirable for people working for the church or Christian organisations to be paid less than the going rate compared to similar secular posts?

_____

_____

_____

3 Are there temptations to favouritism in your relationships?

_____

_____

- Are there groups or individuals you find it hard to treat as generously as others?

_____

_____

- Is gossip and unwarranted criticism a problem in your church? How could it be tackled?

_____

_____

4 How discerning are we about character? Discuss in the group how it might be possible to identify men and women whose sins 'trail behind them'.

_____

_____

- If we suspect someone in leadership of leading a double life, what are the biblical steps to take?

_____

_____

5 What's the leadership style in your church?

_____

_____

- Given the dangers of leadership, shouldn't we prefer a more democratic approach to church life?

_____

_____

6 Pray for your leaders and for young Christians you know who have the gifting to become good leaders.

REVIVAL LIVING

Revival Living
9: Work, words and wealth

1 Timothy 6:1–10

Godliness is a word the world doesn't use. The world speaks about greatness; it will even speak about goodness; but it won't speak about godliness.

Yet godliness is just what should characterise the church. We are supposed to be people who by the grace of God, by the completed work of the Lord Jesus and by the incredible ministry of the Holy Spirit within us and among us, are supposed to demonstrate our holy God in the midst of godlessness.

Paul, significantly, used the word godly (6:3), three times repeated as godliness (6:5,6,11).

The church's responsibility is first to declare God's Word and second to display God's life. And that is precisely what godliness really means. It is a demonstration or display of the life of God.

Two generations ago, a former vicar of St Martin's in the Field Church in London, Canon Dick Shepherd, said, 'The greatest handicap the church has is the unsatisfactory lives of professing Christians'. He was not talking essentially about Christians who swear, lie, cheat or sleep around – but he was talking about the everyday routines of life, about the

> Godliness has a bad press. When you speak of somebody who is godly, you think of somebody who is odd or eccentric … a bit 'off the planet'

REVIVAL LIVING

way that Christians speak to others, the way they handle their wealth and so on. He was talking about the impact of Christians on society.

Godliness has a bad press. When you speak of somebody who is godly, you think of somebody who is odd or eccentric, someone who takes a position and responds to a situation as if they were a bit 'off the planet'.

work situation with the mind of Christ and in the power of the Holy Spirit. This is godliness, alive and well in society.

Masters might be good or bad, harsh and overbearing or considerate and sensitive, rational or totally unreasonable. But Paul says (6:1) that regardless of their character they are to be considered worthy of respect. Sometimes church members find it difficult to respect church leaders; they

> # we don't show the unreasonable boss respect so that we can impress him. We don't do it for our own sake, hoping that knuckling under will make life a bit easier for us. But we do it for God's sake

I am reminded of a poem which deals with this subject. It begins with the sentiment, 'I'd rather see a sermon/ Than hear one any day'. And has the conclusion: 'The best of creatures are the ones/ Who demonstrate their creeds/ For to see good put to action/ Is what everybody needs'. We are living sermons.

Paul's first comments are directed at slaves (6:1,2), but this was no tiny minority. It is estimated that in the Roman Empire there were a staggering 60 million slaves. Two out of every three people who walked the streets of Rome were classified as slaves. Often slaves were humiliated. They could be branded, mistreated, whipped; some were crucified. Yet many were well treated and carried responsibilities within the working world as teachers, doctors, craftsmen and labourers.

Inevitably, the early church had a majority of slaves. The Bible doesn't condone or accept slavery as a system. Scripture recognises that the only thing that will break into human exploitation is to send people into that cultural and

don't understand how their leaders are following the agenda that Jesus has for the congregation. So the natural tendency is to feel ill used and misunderstood, and become critical. If you have a boss in the workplace who is a bit of a bully it's hard to respect him or her. Why should we show respect? Paul tells us that we don't show the unreasonable boss respect so that we can impress him. We don't do it for our own sake, hoping that knuckling under will make life a bit easier for us. But we do it for God's sake, so that God's name and Christian teaching are not slandered.

And when we have a Christian boss (6:2), the great temptation is to be careless. You may even go to the same church as your boss. Familiarity may cause you to become slack, undisciplined, less efficient. Paul counsels against this.

Then Paul, not for the first time in this letter, tackles the area of false doctrine (6:3). He was concerned, of course, about the possibility of error being spoken about the central truths of our faith – the character of God or the person of Jesus or the work of the Spirit, for example. But he was also

REVIVAL LIVING

concerned about other kinds of error, perhaps more subtle and yet easily promoted, even within churches. Some of the wrong teachings I have heard over the years include things like 'Everyone must speak in tongues' or 'Communal living is the highest form of spirituality' or 'Prophecy is more important than Scripture'. I have heard people say 'God will heal everyone'. I have heard 'The ultimate authority for Christians is the church meeting'. I have been told 'God wants to make you rich, financially'.

Some of these things sound attractive, but they are not what the Bible teaches. Godliness is about accepting and acting on the Word of God as it comes to us in the power of the Spirit through the Scriptures. That is normative for Christian living.

I have had the privilege of meeting many godly people. If there is one characteristic every one of them holds in common it is their contentment. Whether they have little or much of this world's goods and power, they are happy with their lot. Hands full or hands empty, stomach full or hungry, they are content. They have understood that life is not fastened to the things we have to leave behind. There are no pockets in a shroud.

Two men were at a bus stop, discussing a third who had died recently and had been extremely rich. One said 'How much did he leave?' The second fellow replied, 'Everything!' We can take nothing with us.

But there's not just the **death of the body** to consider, but the **desire of the mind**. Paul says that rich people are

godly people … have understood that life is not fastened to the things we have to leave behind. There are no pockets in a shroud

Leading theologian and writer Jim Packer says, 'Loyalty to Christ our risen Saviour and Lord calls for total submission to Scripture and anyone or any church declining to believe and do what is written or failing in practice to be faithful to it is to that extent a rebel against Christ'. That's pretty strong stuff! But this is biblical and the Bible is revelation of the heart of God!

Those who promote false teaching are identifiable by the characteristics Paul lists (6:4). They are conceited and contentious, always at the heart of something that is disruptive and destructive and damaging to the body of Jesus Christ. And Paul says they are covetous. They are out for what they can get – whether that's money or position or control or recognition.

So godliness is about our **work** and about our **words**. And, finally, it is about our **wealth** (6:6-10).

prone to temptation (6:9). Epicurus, a philosopher who lived many centuries ago, said, 'The secret of contentment is not to add to a man's possessions but to take away from his desires'. A content person is not always wanting.

From the **death of the body** and the **desire of the mind**, Paul moves on to the **destruction of the soul**. Actually, money can bring all kinds of good. Money feeds the hungry, clothes the naked, provides medicine for the sick, gives shelter to the homeless. Money can be a blessing. But Paul says (6:10) that the love of money is the root of all kinds of evil. For money Delilah betrayed Samson to the Philistines. For money Ananias and Sapphira became the first hypocrites in the Christian church and lost their lives. For money Judas sold Christ and was ruined eternally. Surely these human tragedies speak loudly and eloquently.

WORKSHEET

Revival Living Worksheet

9: Work, words and wealth

1 Timothy 6:1–10

1 Is there someone you know who you would describe as 'godly'? Describe the characteristics of that person that prompt the use of that word.

_____

_____

_____

2 Where do you most experience difficulties in respecting those in authority over you? In the workplace? In the church? Elsewhere?

_____

_____

- How do we make sense of 6:1 in our culture of employee's rights?

_____

_____

_____

3 What false teachings are prevalent today?

_____

_____

- What are the antidotes?

_____

_____

4 What particular attacks on striving for godliness are there in a very affluent society?

_____

_____

- And in a very poor one?

_____

_____

5 How have you personally struggled with knowing what is 'enough'?

_____

_____

_____

6 'The secret of contentment is not to add to a man's possessions but to take away from his desires' (Epicurus). What do you think of this view?

_____

_____

- Are our desires to be eliminated or moderated? How?

_____

_____

7 Spend some time praying for a fairer distribution of the world's wealth.

REVIVAL LIVING

Revival Living
10: Aiming high
1 Timothy 6:11–22

Throughout this whole letter, Paul, now an ageing apostle, is urging the young Timothy to aim high in his Christian walk, not to settle for mediocrity but to be the very best he can be for God.

Having described many ungodly ways of behaving in the first part of chapter 6, Paul here moves on to encourage Timothy to be different, to follow the example of Jesus, and to look to Jesus as the standard for real Christian living.

Comparison is very important in our society, but the great shame is that instead of comparing ourselves with Jesus or right-living people we are constantly tempted to comparisons with the wrong people.

Who you compare yourself with matters a great deal. Perhaps you see others behaving dishonestly or unkindly in the workplace and you don't see that you should behave differently. Perhaps other Christians you know don't turn up to events or don't read their Bibles or can't be bothered to witness. So why should you? But Paul's encouragement to Timothy, in effect, is 'Never mind what others do, you be different. Don't settle for less, rise above their standards'. The church is full of people who have settled for the

A James Bond or a Stallone charges into danger to rescue a nation, shrugging off bullets with ease… Having fallen off buildings and been blown up in a car, he walks out of the smoke haze, slightly sweating but otherwise totally intact, and with enough energy to make love to the beautiful heroine. Amazing!

mediocrity of their peers. But God is calling us beyond that, to be men and women prepared to be different and better.

Paul begins by reminding Timothy that he is a man of God (6:11). That's exactly where many of us need to start to change things in our lives, by reminding ourselves that Jesus lives in us and that we are men and women of God who need to become who we are. Yes, life is full of desperate problems – but we are children of the King!

A story is told about Napoleon, the great French general, who had a soldier brought up before him on a charge. The first thing Napoleon said to the soldier was, 'Soldier, what is your name?' The soldier, with some embarrassment, said, 'My name is Napoleon'. He had the same name as the general. The general just looked at him and said, 'Change your behaviour – or change your name'. He just didn't want bad behaviour associated with his name.

When we behave badly, we are not only denying who we really are in Christ, but also damaging the name of Christ. Even in our relationships to one another, we need to learn to build each other up rather than being negative. In British culture it is quite acceptable, particularly in humour, to tear others down. We need to stop using negative language and affirm one another as men and women of God, aspiring to live our destiny. We want to live a God-intoxicated life, because we belong to him.

But notice (6:11) that sometimes to be a hero you have to run away. What does Timothy need to flee from? From all the dangers and temptations outlined in the first 10 verses of the chapter. The world's heroes don't run away. A James Bond or a Stallone charges into danger to rescue a nation, shrugging off bullets with ease. People fall in dozens around our hero with a blaze of a gun, a flick of a knife or a punch of the fist. Having fallen off buildings and been blown up in a car, he walks out of the smoke haze, slightly sweating but otherwise totally intact, and with enough energy to make love to the beautiful heroine. Amazing! And totally unreal – because sometimes real heroes run away.

One of the features of postmodernity is the provisional nature of loyalty

In the adrenaline rush of ministry, sometimes a Christian is tempted to be heroic in a confrontational sense – but some things should be run from. Sometimes we think we are stronger than we really are as Christians, and we sail close to the wind, exposing ourselves to temptations. We need to learn the common sense to run from sin. It's not cowardice to avoid danger – it's wisdom. The true hero knows when to run from what's wrong and run towards righteousness.

In the next verse (6:12) Paul is calling Timothy to remember his baptism or his ordination. He is being asked to recall the form of words he made as his good confession. He made certain promises in front of others and should now recall that commitment.

This is really appropriate for our own culture. One of the features of postmodernity is the provisional nature of loyalty. Too many people promise something one day and then go back on it the next because they think they've had a better offer. That is why marriage is under such threat. Couples line up in churches on Saturdays in the decent weather between April and September to make vows to each other, and serious promises in front of God and within the legal system, and within months many have abandoned those promises. They meant nothing! When promises become inconvenient we abandon them wholesale. Life moves on.

Paul reminds Timothy that he promised to fight the good fight, and that Christian discipleship is a life-long commitment to God, with no exclusion clause that when life gets hard you can give up on it.

REVIVAL LIVING

I trained at Spurgeon's Theological College in South London. The college crest is a little Latin phrase with two hands holding on to a Cross. The Latin phrase means 'I hold and am held'. I am holding on to the Cross and the Cross is holding on to me. I hold on to God and God holds on to me. This is Paul's encouragement to Timothy, to hold on, living out his promises, while God will hold into him.

It's God, of course, who is the audience of One (6:14) for whom we live and do everything. We all tend to modify our behaviour depending on who's watching. If I am undressing in the bedroom and my wife's there I am more likely to hang my clothes up! If she is absent I am less likely to do that. Before you feel too smug, I challenge you to think about the way you, too, change what you do depending on who's watching.

The thing is, God really is present with us all the time! Not to nag or condemn us – but to support and affirm us. So living our lives with an audience of One shouldn't be a threat, but an enormous encouragement. God the Father, who knows us better than anyone and loves us in spite of all our weaknesses, wants our ministry to succeed and our lives to succeed. That's why we can aim high, conscious of his presence and conscious that Jesus might come again any second. Paul reminds Timothy (6:15,16) of the magnificence and greatness of God in heaven. That vision will give Timothy a different perspective. Thousands of Christians live with the perspective of the gutter. But God's perspective is the towering overview. That perspective reveals that God alone is in charge of history. His all-seeing view of my ministry is what matters, not my view from the gutter. His view of me is more important than my view of me. This releases me from the pressures and anxieties of ministry and enables me to rise above them.

Ephesus was an incredibly affluent city, a rich trading post on the western edge of the Asian empire and a leaping-off point into Europe. There were rich Romans, rich Greeks, rich Jewish traders there.

In the ancient world there was really no middle class. Slaves, as we have seen, were a huge percentage of the population. And then there were the rich. Young Timothy, as the pastor, finds himself in a dilemma. In his congregation are slaves and land-owning wealthy traders. Nothing breeds division in a church like envy, and Paul knows that.

Many churches face similar stresses. In many congregations there are those who are rich materially, and those who struggle to make ends meet. Of course, in absolute terms, every single member of every congregation in the western world is rich. We are all loaded. We are affluent beyond the wildest dreams of 75 per cent of the people on the planet. By global standards we are rich. But, in comparative terms, some of us are richer than others. We have different standards of homes, cars and other possessions. But materialism is just as much a terrible cancer in today's culture as it was for the Ephesians.

To some degree the rich/poor divide will cause heartaches for any pastor. Sometimes just one or two families in a small church hold the purse strings and can use their influence for their own ends. So Paul warns Timothy to watch out for wealthy people seeking power and control. Of course, his livelihood may actually depend on those same people. But the danger for rich people is that they become unbelievably arrogant. We see it often reflected in stories in the newspapers. Rich people can become totally cavalier about the law and other peoples' feelings.

Because we we have missed Don't settle for second best!

REVIVAL LIVING

The great danger is that when we are rich and affluent, as most of us are, we don't need to trust God for our future because we have got the right investments or the right savings plan or the right share options. We don't need to trust God because everything's sown up materially. Imagine having enough money so that when you become old and infirm you can go to the best old people's home anywhere and live there comfortably for 40 years on the money you have got. Your children and spouse are provided for and there is money left over. Wouldn't the temptation be to be casual about your relationship with God? Why would you need to trust him?

But if you lived in a part of the world where you weren't sure where your next meal was coming from, you would not be so casual. Nor would you be if you were sick and the nearest doctor was 100 miles away. Your prayer life would have an edge of urgency. Need produces dependence.

It's not that material things are wrong in themselves. But they are not ultimately satisfying, and do not guarantee happiness or eternal security. The responsibility of the rich is to use their blessings generously for the benefit of all; and the responsibility of the poorer among us is to avoid the sins of envy and jealousy.

The Bible is quite clear that genuine enjoyment is about abandonment to God. That is the antidote to materialism – not some vague spirituality but a great passion arising among us. So often we have bought into the materialism of the day and we live like pagans while at the same time proclaiming our Christian faith. What a testimony to Jesus a generous, sharing church community is!

> every single member of every congregation in the western world is rich. We are all loaded

When I was a student I went to a posh meal where the first course was soup and rolls and I took the opportunity to have second and third helpings, not realising that there were many more courses to come. By the time I got to the third course I was totally full and quite embarrassed at having to leave so much wonderful food on my plate. What really worries me about the church is that thousands of us are settling for the soup course and we have never feasted where God wants us to feast. Because we are so absorbed by the little things we have missed the big thing God has for us. Don't settle for second best! Take Paul's advice: guard the truth (6:20) and keep the faith.

> are so absorbed by the little things
> the big thing God has for us.

WORKSHEET

Revival Living Worksheet

10: Aiming high

1 Timothy 6:11–22

1 Is 6:11 appropriate advice for young men and women of faith today?

_____
_____
_____

2 What incentives does Paul offer Timothy for doing his best for God?

_____
_____

• Are these motivations which make sense for people today?

_____
_____

3 What particular barriers are there in our society to being 'sold out' for God?

_____
_____
_____

4 Is the church distinctive enough in our society?

_____
_____

• How can the church become a more radical community that will attract others?

_____
_____

5 Are there any practical steps you can suggest as to how we can encourage the sharing described in 6:18?

_____
_____

6 As advice from a mentor, how valuable do you think Paul's letter to Timothy really is?

_____
_____

• How can we promote good mentoring relationships within the church to benefit younger Christians?

_____
_____

7 Look at the last four words of the chapter. Why are these so important?

_____
_____
_____

8 Review together the truths from 1 Timothy that have made most impact on each of you. Pray for the Holy Spirit to help you guard the truth and keep the faith.

the Word made fresh! -

other titles from Stephen Gaukroger

Transition Living

insights from 1 Samuel for the 3rd millennium church

From the big picture of international politics and business right through to the daily routines of individuals in our planet's many and varied nations, the current agenda is typically one of massive change – and the climate a loss of confidence and equilibrium. Culturally, many parts of western society face moral decline, and family and community meltdown.

Have we been here before? Are there lessons to learn from the past? The days of Old Tes-tament giants Samuel, Saul and David were similarly unsettled, as the 12 tribes of Israel struggled with the transition to nationhood. There are principles and parallels here to impact us personally and nationally on our faith journeys.

ISBN 1 84427 040 8

A Code for Living

the Ten Commandments for the 3rd millennium church

Largely forgotten – yet hugely foundational. Dismissed by many as ancient rules irrelevant today, the Ten Commandments are of vital and practical importance to the way society operates, providing an essential framework for how we relate to God and to each other in fulfilling ways.

But aren't they a 'mission impossible'? True, none of us can keep all the commandments all the time. The only way to obey these laws is through a new power and a new heart that's part of knowing Jesus. We need to rediscover why the Ten Commandments are so potentially enriching to us as individuals and communities.

ISBN 1 84427 041 6

Available from Christian bookshops or from Scripture Union Mail Order:
PO Box 5148, Milton Keynes MLO, MK2 2YX, tel 01908 856006 or online through www.scriptureunion.org.uk

church@home

SU's online magazine for the world of small groups

• ready-to-use sessions to try • inspirational articles • 'how to' features

• case studies on real groups • reports of best practice • your space for your say

• info on training and resources

www.scriptureunion.org.uk/churchathome

the one-stop shop for all your small group needs

Other small group resources from SCRIPTURE UNION

CONNECT BIBLE STUDIES

Innovative small groups studies that help interpret contemporary culture in the light of Biblical insights. Engage with popular books, TV programmes, music and film. Four themes, four sessions in each.

Over 20 titles available, including:

Harry Potter	Lord of the Rings
The Matrix	The Simpsons
Billy Elliot	James Bond 007
TV Game Shows	Friends
Madonna	John Grisham's Thrillers

A JOURNEY OF THE HEART

THE PILGRIM'S GUIDE TO PRAYER

Kate Hayes

Do you find prayer a welcome time of personal space? A tedious duty? An adventure? An embarrassment? A struggle with concentration? Uplifting? Confusing? Intimidating?

Do you see it as a skill to be practised? An art to perfect? An exercise to be endured? As natural as breathing? As tricky as skateboarding?

If you want to explore what it means to pray with purpose, growing in understanding of and intimacy with your God, this series of six Bible-based studies – which can be tackled in a small group or on your own – will take you on a rewarding journey.

Ideal for Lent – but great at other times, too! Includes sections on:

* praying alone
* praying with and for others
* praying about difficult decisions
* praying in the tough times
* fasting

ISBN 1 85999 797 X

These and many other small group resources from Scripture Union are available from Christian bookshops or from Scripture Union Mail Order: PO Box 5148, Milton Keynes MLO, MK2 2YX, tel 01908 856006 or online through www.scriptureunion.org.uk

SCRIPTURE UNION
USING THE BIBLE TO INSPIRE CHILDREN, YOUNG PEOPLE AND ADULTS TO KNOW GOD